TELL ME HOW IT WORKS

# HOW DO DRONES WORK?

DANIEL R. FAUST

PowerKiDS press

New York

Published in 2021 by The Rosen Publishing Group, Inc.
29 East 21st Street, New York, NY 10010

First Edition

Editor: Siyavush Saidian
Book Design: Reann Nye

Photo Credits: Cover LALS STOCK/Shutterstock.com; Series Art (gears) goodwin_x/Shutterstock.com; Series Art (newspaper) Here/Shutterstock.com; p. 5 Jacob Lund/Shutterstock.com; p. 6 https://commons.wikimedia.org/wiki/File:Teledyne-Ryan-Firebee-hatzerim-1.jpg; p. 7 TASS/Getty Images; p. 9 Valentin Valkov/Shutterstock.com; p. 11 (top) RikoBest/Shutterstock.com; p. 11 (bottom) Andy Dean Photography/Shutterstock.com; p. 13 (top) Artie Medvedev/Shutterstock.com; p. 13 (bottom) Ethan Miller/Getty Images News/Getty Images; p. 15 (top) Denis Belitsky/Shutterstock.com; p. 15 (bottom) aapsky/Shutterstock.com; p. 17 (background) kzww/Shutterstock.com; p. 17 (drone) Alexander Kolomietz/Shutterstock.com; p. 18 https://commons.wikimedia.org/wiki/File:556th_RS_AQM-34_Drone.jpg; p. 19 Smith Collection/Gado/Archive Photos/Getty Images; p. 21 baranozdemir/E+/Getty Images; p. 22 Alex Yuzhakov/Shutterstock.com.

Library of Congress Cataloging-in-Publication Data

Names: Faust, Daniel R., author.
Title: How do drones work? / Daniel R. Faust.
Description: New York : PowerKids Press, [2021] | Series: Tell me how it works | Includes bibliographical references and index.
Identifiers: LCCN 2019052448 | ISBN 9781725318137 (paperback) | ISBN 9781725318151 (library binding) | ISBN 9781725318144  (6 pack)
Subjects: LCSH: Drone aircraft–Juvenile literature.
Classification: LCC TL685.35 .F38 2021 | DDC 629.133/39–dc23
LC record available at https://lccn.loc.gov/2019052448

Manufactured in the United States of America

CPSIA Compliance Information: Batch #CWPK20. For Further Information contact Rosen Publishing, New York, New York at 1-800-237-9932.

Find us on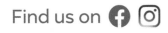

# CONTENTS

# LOOK! UP IN THE SKY!

In December 2018, hundreds of flights at Gatwick Airport in London, England, were canceled following reports of drones being sighted near the runway. In January of the following year, flights were **disrupted** at Newark Airport in New Jersey over drone sightings.

It seems like it's impossible to follow the news today without seeing stories about drones, whether they're responsible for closing down airports or being used in war. It's not hard to see that drones are everywhere.

Drones are best used in wide open outside spaces. It's against the law to fly a drone near an airport.

# WHAT IS A DRONE?

When people talk about drones, they're usually talking about unmanned aerial vehicles, or UAVs. A UAV is a type of aircraft that operates without an onboard pilot. UAVs are controlled by either a built-in computer or by a pilot on the ground using a handheld machine called a remote control.

6

Built in 1951, the Ryan Firebee was one of the first jet-powered drones. Militaries around the world use similar drones today to help train gunners.

**TECH TALK**

Many UGVs look like small tanks or remote-controlled cars. The military uses them to search for **mines** and other unsafe materials and gather information about an area before troops arrive.

Although UAVs are the most common type of drone, not all drones fly. Like their flying cousins, unmanned ground vehicles, or UGVs, are operated remotely. There are even aquatic drones called unmanned underwater vehicles, or UUVs.

# BUILDING A DRONE

Drones can come in many different shapes and sizes. However, they all have the same basic **components**. Every drone has a frame, or body. It also has a power source, a flight controller, sensors, and a means of **propulsion**.

A drone's frame is usually built out of plastics or lightweight metals, such as aluminum. The lighter a drone is, the less power it will need to move. A battery gives the drone the power it needs to fly.

# WHAT A DRONE IS MADE OF

**PROPELLERS**

**BODY/ FRAME**

**SENSORS**

**POWER SOURCE/ BATTERY**

**CAMERA**

**FLIGHT CONTROLLER**

The most common type of drone available to the public is the quadcopter, named for its four helicopter-like propellers.

9

The controller—or flight computer—is the drone's brain. The controller receives input from the drone's flier. It controls the drone's speed and direction, and it can even allow the drone to fly by itself.

The final basic component is the drone's sensor. Sensors provide information about the drone's surroundings and alert the drone if it's about to collide with, or crash into, an object. GPS allows the drone operator to track the drone and know its exact location at all times. Video cameras allow the drone's operator to see whatever the drone "sees."

**TECH TALK**

Some drones have highly advanced sensors. Military drones, for example, have **infrared** and night-vision cameras that allow them to operate at night or in bad weather.

HOUSE SEEN THROUGH HEAT-SENSING DRONE

DRONE SENSOR POD

DANGER

Some drones have sensors that can find the heat given off by people and things. Law enforcement officials, such as police, can use these drones to locate escaped criminals or to find people lost in the wilderness.

11

# TAKING TO THE SKIES

Although all drones are operated from a distance, the devices used to control them can vary. Most small drones, like common quadcopters, are operated by handheld controllers that look like video game controllers.

Some military drones are operated with handheld controllers too. Others are operated using portable, or easy to move, consoles that look like laptops. Larger military drones, like the MQ-9 Reaper or the RQ-4 Global Hawk, are controlled from large, stationary consoles that look like airplane cockpits.

**TECH TALK**

There's an app for that! That's right, some high-end drones can be flown using Wi-Fi with nothing more than an app on your smartphone or tablet.

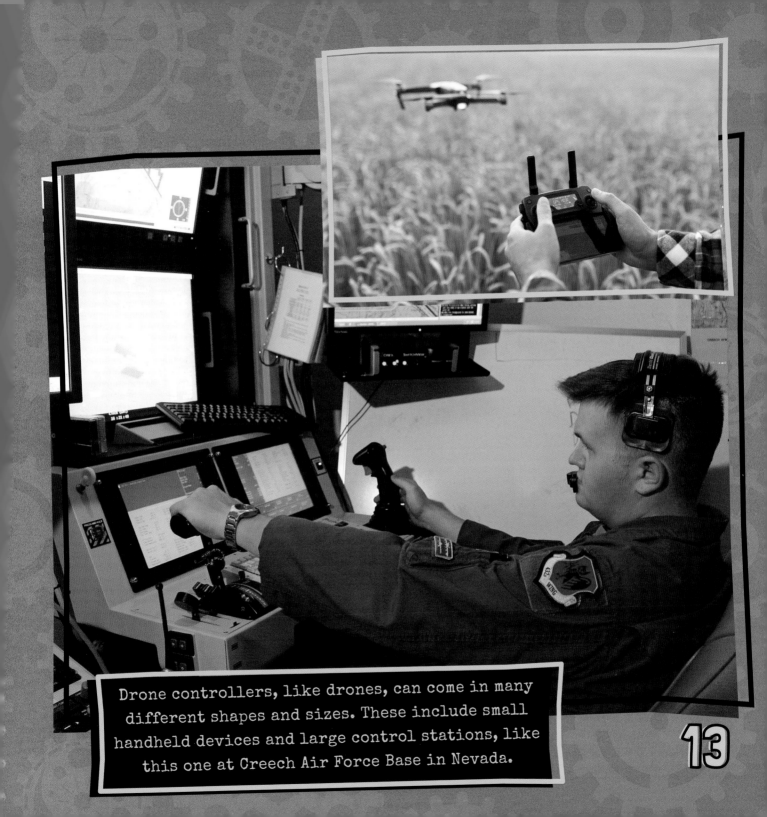

Drone controllers, like drones, can come in many different shapes and sizes. These include small handheld devices and large control stations, like this one at Creech Air Force Base in Nevada.

13

# WINGS AND ROTORS

Drones can be as large as a jet plane or small enough to fit in the palm of your hand. Whatever their size, most drones belong to one of two groups. A drone can be a fixed-wing aircraft or it can be a rotor-wing aircraft.

Fixed-wing drones look just like the average airplane. They have two fixed, or stationary, wings on the body and **stabilizers** on the back of the aircraft. These drones are pushed forward by propellers or jet engines, causing the air to flow over and under the wings. This creates the lift the drone needs to get off the ground.

**JET PLANE**

**FIXED-WING DRONE**

All fixed-wing aircraft have the same basic design. Can you see the similarities between this drone and this jet plane? Can you locate the wings and stabilizers on both aircraft?

Rotor-wing drones resemble rotorcraft, like helicopters. Rotorcraft have special wings called rotor blades that rotate around a mast, or central pole, at great speeds. This rotation is what creates the lift needed for the rotorcraft to rise into the air. The wings are also curved on top and flat on the bottom, meaning air flows faster over the top. This also creates lift.

Most casual users fly rotor-wing drones. They're easy to use and cheap to buy. Military and police groups use both fixed-wing and rotor-wing drones.

## TECH TALK

Aircraft fly because they're built to balance four forces. Thrust is the force that moves an aircraft forward. Drag tries to slow the aircraft down. Weight is the force caused by the pull of gravity. Lift is the force that holds the aircraft in the air.

# DRONE FORCES

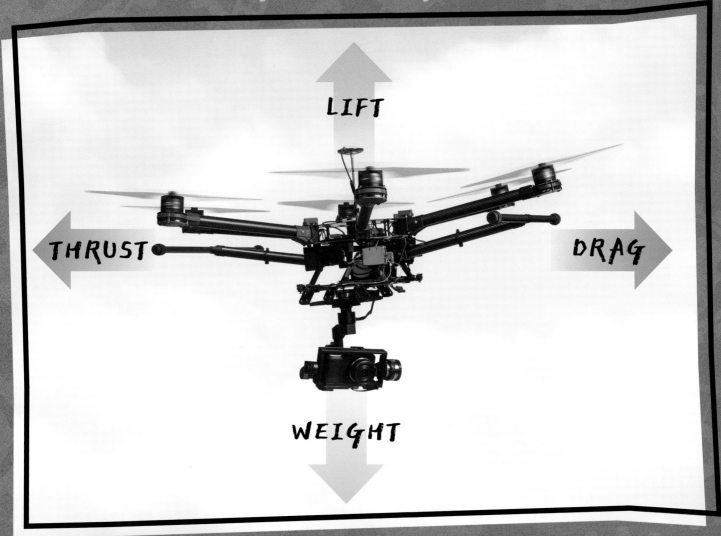

LIFT

THRUST

DRAG

WEIGHT

Lift, weight, thrust, and drag work in opposite pairs. Lift raises the aircraft while weight pulls it down. Thrust works against drag, which tries to prevent the aircraft from moving forward.

# MANY MISSIONS

Flying drones can be a lot of fun, but these devices are also being used to perform a growing number of serious tasks. The military started using drones for **reconnaissance** missions, or tasks, on a large scale around the time of the Vietnam War.

EARLY MILITARY RECONNAISSANCE DRONE

Larger drones can stay in the air longer and fly higher than smaller drones. The RQ-4 Global Hawk has a wingspan of 131 feet (39.9 m). It can fly missions that last longer than 30 hours, and can fly as high as 60,000 feet (18,288 m).

Many of the drones the military uses today are still used to safely gather information. Unmanned combat aerial vehicles, or UCAVs, carry bombs, or explosives. Combat drones are used to destroy enemy camps.

19

There are many nonmilitary uses for drones as well. Drones are often used after natural disasters, or harmful natural events, to search for survivors. They can also be used to bring water and medical supplies, such as drugs, to people trapped in hard-to-reach areas.

Scientists are studying weather patterns and exploring the ocean depths with the help of drones. Animal rights groups use drones to monitor wild animals and track **poachers**. Engineers can use drones to check buildings, bridges, and other structures for damage.

### TECH TALK

Drones are changing jobs in film and photography. A quadcopter equipped with a digital camera is cheaper and safer than using larger aircraft like helicopters for aerial photography.

Farmers use drones to inspect their fields and identify the areas that need attention. Ranchers can use drones to monitor their herds or search for missing animals.

21

# DRONES OF TOMORROW

Drones are here to stay. As drone parts become more advanced, drones may become more common in our everyday lives. Whether or not the skies overhead become filled with drones, the real **future** of drones may lie out in space.

Drone shuttles are being used to deliver cargo to the International Space Station, where astronauts are using drones to help keep things running smoothly. NASA even has plans to send drones to explore the faraway moons and planets of our solar system!

# GLOSSARY

**component:** Part of a mechanical or electrical system.

**disrupt:** To cause something to be unable to continue in the normal way.

**future:** The events that happen after the present time.

**infrared:** Referring to rays of light that can't be seen and are longer than rays that produce red light.

**mine:** A bomb placed on the ground that blows up when touched.

**poacher:** A person who catches or kills animals illegally.

**propulsion:** The force that moves something forward.

**reconnaissance:** The exploration of a place to collect information.

**stabilizer:** The part of an airplane's tail that maintains control and stability.

23

## WEBSITES

24 Due to the changing nature of Internet links, PowerKids Press has developed an online list of websites related to the subject of this book. This site is updated regularly. Please use this link to access the list: www.powerkidslinks.com/tmhiw/drones